ROBERT KAHN

BOBBY
and
MANDEE'S
Bike Safety

To order additional copies of this book, contact:
Xlibris
1-888-795-4274
www.Xlibris.com
Orders@Xlibris.com

ISBN: Softcover   978-1-7960-9877-8
       EBook   978-1-7960-9876-1

Print information available on the last page

Rev. date: 05/29/2020

BOBBY
and
MANDEE'S
Bike Safety

Hello, I'm Bobby and this is my sister Mandee. In this book we are going to talk about being safe while riding our bikes.

Once a week check your bike to make sure it is safe. Look at the chain and make sure it is oiled and correctly adjusted.

Check the hand brake and that the brake pads are in good condition. If you have a coaster brake, make sure that it is working correctly.

Make sure that all bolts are not loose, but snug. Also make sure that the handlebar is secure.

And be sure that the rims aren't bent and securely in place. At least once a year, take your bike to a bike shop and have the spokes adjusted or replaced if needed.

Check that the reflectors are still in place on the front and the back of your bike. There should also be reflectors on the pedals. You may want to put reflectors also on the spokes.

If you have a front and a rear light, check that they are working. Also if you have a bell, or a horn, check that it is working.

Check that the tires are properly inflated. Make sure that there isn't too much, or not enough air, is in them. And make sure that the seat is in place and tight.

Also make sure that it is adjusted to your height. You should be able to place your feet flat on the ground while you're sitting on the seat.

Now that the bike is safe, let's make you safe. Always wear a bike helmet that fits you correctly.

There are over 300,000 children treated in hospital emergency rooms for bicycle related injuries every year.

Hey Mandee, about 85% of bike injuries could have been prevented if children had worn their helmets

Left Turn

Right Turn

Stop

Mandee we are now ready to talk about the safety rules of riding your bike.

First let's review the proper hand signals.

To make a left turn, you hold your arm straight out.

Here is the correct signal for a right turn. Your arm is bent at the elbow and the forearm is up.

And the correct hand signal for stopping is your left arm is away from your body and pointed down.

Most bikes are made to only have "1 Rider" on it. Don't give friends a ride when you are riding your bike.

Also don't carry articles in your arms. This will interfere with the proper control and balance of your riding. Always keep both hands on the handle bars.

Mandee, let's go for a bike ride to our older sister Laura's. I'll teach you about the safety rules for riding a bike.

First we look left, right, and left again before leaving our driveway and entering the street. Since there aren't any cars coming, let's go. Remember Mandee, always keep watching for on coming traffic.

If you ride a tricycle, or are still really small, then you should ride on the sidewalk.

Always ride your bike in a safe and courteous manner. Also remember that pedestrians have the right of way. This important rule is for riding on the sidewalk or in the street.

Mandee, ride on the right side of the street and ride in the same direction as the traffic is going.

We have to turn right onto Main Street, show the hand signal for a right hand turn.

That was awesome Mandee.

Look there is a parked car that we have to ride around.

I will tell you what to do. Look behind you over your left shoulder. Always look over the left shoulder since that is the side closest to traffic.

If cars are coming down the street, use the slowing down hand signal. If you have to stop, "STOP" behind the parked car at the side of the road.

Let the cars pass by you and the parked car. Then look again over your left shoulder. When it is clear, and there isn't any traffic coming, ride around the parked car.

Once you have passed the parked car, move back over closer to the side of the road.

Mandee at the end of this block, we have to cross the street.

First we will obey the Stop Sign and "STOP" at the corner.

Now we will get off of our bikes. Next we'll look both ways and make sure that there aren't any cars coming. Always look to the left then to the right and then check again to the left for traffic.

If a car is at the cross walk, always make sure the driver of the car sees you. When it is clear, we will walk our bikes across the street in the cross walk.

36

Now that we made it across the street, make sure it is safe before you get back on your bike. Look over your left shoulder for traffic. Is it clear? OK let's go.

Look we are coming to a Yield Sign. Mandee what does it mean to Yield? That's right. If traffic is coming we have to slow down, or stop. Then we let the traffic go first before we can continue.

Look there is Laura waiting for us. We have to make a left turn into her driveway. Use the signal for a left turn. Check for traffic driving up and down the street. Is it clear? Yes, then let's turn into her driveway.

Mandee that was an excellent bike ride. On the way home, I want you to give me the instructions for riding our bikes safely.

Come on, let's go and give Laura a hug and visit with her.

QUESTIONS

1. How often should you inspect your bike to make sure it is safe?

answer on page 2

2. What do you need to wear everytime you ride your bike?

answer on page 7

3. Is it ok to wear a helmet that doesn't fit correctly?

answer on page 7

4. Show a left turn hand signal.

answer on page 8

5. How many children are treated each year because they didn't wear a helmet?

answer on page 7

6. Show the hand signal for slowing down or stopping.

answer on page 8

7. Show a right turn hand signal.

answer on page 8

8. When you're riding your bicycle is it ok to have more than 1 person on the bike?

answer on page 9

9. Is it all right to ride your bike while you're carrying articles in your hands?

answer page 9

10. Is it all right to ride your bike using only one hand on the handlebar?

answer page 9

11. If you ride a tricycle, or are still small, where should you ride?

answer on page 11

12. Who always has the right of way?

answer on page 11

13. Before riding out of a driveway, what should you do?

answer on page 12

14. Which side of the street should you ride on and why?

answer on page 13

15. What do you need to do before riding around a parked car?

answer on pages 15&16

16. What if a car is coming behind you when you look?

answer on page 16

17. Once the car, or cars, have passed, what should you do?

answer on page 17

18. When you have passed the parked car, what should you do?

answer on page 17

19. Do bike riders have to stop at a STOP Sign?

answer on page 18

20. You're going to cross at a crosswalk, what is the first thing you should do?

STOP   AND   _____   _____

_____ _____

Then LOOK _____ _____

Then WALK _____ _____ across the street in the crosswalk.

answers on page 19

21. Tell what a yield sign means and what you should do when you're riding your bike? answer on page 21

Printed in the United States
By Bookmasters